Day and Night

Kay Davies
and
Wendy Oldfield

Wayland

Starting Science

Books in the series

Animals
Day and Night
Electricity and Magnetism
Floating and Sinking
Food
Hot and Cold
Information Technology
Light
Local Ecology
Materials

Plants
Pushing and Pulling
Rocks and Soil
The Senses
Skeletons and Movement
Sound and Music
Time and Change
Waste
Water
Weather

About this book

This book investigates how the Earth in space travels around the Sun, to give us a continuous succession of days and nights. Children learn different methods of telling the time, and discover how other animals and plants plan their lives around daytime and night-time.

Day and Night provides an introduction to science enquiry methods. The activities and investigations are designed to be straightforward but fun, and flexible according to the abilities of the children. Through them, the children use a variety of ways to explore the world around them.

The full-page picture in each chapter, with its commentary, may be taken as a focal point for further discussion or as an introduction to the topic. Each chapter can form a basis for extended topic work.

Teachers will find that in using this book, they are reinforcing the other core subjects of language and mathematics. Through its topic approach, Day and Night covers aspects of the National Science Curriculum for key stage 1 (levels 1 to 3), for the following Attainment Targets: Exploration of science (AT1), The variety of life (AT2), and The Earth in space (AT16).

First published in 1992 by
Wayland (Publishers) Ltd
61 Western Road, Hove
East Sussex BN3 1JD, England

© Copyright 1992 Wayland (Publishers) Ltd

Typeset by Kalligraphic Design Ltd, Horley, Surrey
Printed in Italy by Rotolito Lombarda S.p.A., Milan
Bound in Belgium by Casterman S.A.

British Library Cataloguing in Publication Data
Davies, Kay
    Day and night. – (Starting science)
    I. Title   II. Oldfield, Wendy   III. Series
372.3

ISBN 0 7502 0311 0

Book editor: Joanna Housley
Series editor: Cally Chambers

CONTENTS

Are you awake? 5

Dawn to dusk 6

Marking time 9

Sands of time 11

Time on my hands 12

Strike a light 14

Moonshine 17

Time tactics 18

Nightspot 21

Night patrol 23

Open and shut case 25

Star bright 26

Sleep tight 29

Glossary 30

Finding out more 31

Index 32

All words that first appear in **bold** in the text are explained in the glossary.

The cockerel is awake at first light in the morning.
He crows loudly and everyone knows it is the start of
a new day.

ARE YOU AWAKE?

Did you know that the Earth we live on is moving?
It is! It is moving in space around the Sun.
The Earth takes one year to travel round the Sun.
The Sun stays still but its light reaches us on Earth.
The Earth spins as it travels.
Each spin takes one day to complete.
Every day everywhere on Earth has some daytime and
some night-time.

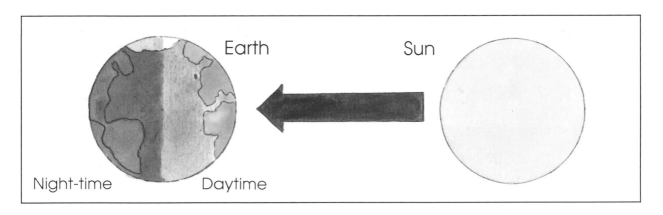

Earth   Sun

Night-time   Daytime

Ask a friend to hold a lighted torch in a dark room.
The torch is the Sun.

Hold a globe of the Earth so that the light from the torch shines on it.
Spin the globe slowly.
Look for daytime and night-time on the Earth.

DAWN TO DUSK

Sunlight makes our Earth look bright and colourful. Anything that blocks the light casts a **shadow**.

Find a sunny window.

Notice where the Sun is in the sky.

Stick a dark shape on to a pane of glass.

Look for where the shadow falls on the floor. Stick a piece of paper on to the floor and draw round the shadow.
Do this every half-hour.

Does the shadow move? Is the Sun in the same place when you start and finish your investigation?

Don't stare at the Sun – it can damage your eyes.

On a sunny day there are shadows everywhere.
They make shapes on the ground and walls.

A **sundial** can tell us the time. The lines show where shadows fall at different times of the day.

MARKING TIME

Stand a tall post in the middle of the playground. Tie 3 m of string to the post.

Tie chalk to the other end of the string and draw a circle on the playground.

Mark the spot where the post's shadow crosses the circle.
Write in the time.

Ask your friends to put markers where they think the shadow will fall an hour later.

Whose mark is nearest?

Mark the shadow and time each hour on the circle.

Can you use your shadow clock to tell the time the next day?

The sand falls through a hole in the egg timer.
It takes five minutes to empty the top glass.

SANDS OF TIME

We cannot use the Sun to tell us the time at night.
We have learnt to use other ways to measure time.

Cut a plastic bottle in half.
Cover the neck with plastic film.
Make a small hole in the film.
Fit the neck into the bottom of the bottle.
Fill the top with dry sand.
Use a watch to see how long it takes to fall through.

Find out about other timers. How do they work?

TIME ON MY HANDS

There are twenty-four hours in each day.
We can measure this time in two periods: twelve hours before noon and twelve hours after noon.
We can also use a twenty-four hour clock.
This follows the hours throughout the whole day.

Stick a clock face on a square of card.

Copy the extra numbers, from 13 to 24, round the edge like this.

Put an hour hand and a minute hand on your clock.

Morning times are on your round clock.
Afternoon and evening times are on your square clock.

Some **digital timers** use the twenty-four hour clock.
Are these times in the morning or afternoon?

The figures on this clock strike the hours.
Clocks can have two hands to tell us the time in hours
and minutes.

STRIKE A LIGHT

In most parts of the world days and nights are not always the same length.
Days are longer than nights in summer.
They are shorter than nights in winter.
At night-time it can be dangerous if we cannot see properly.

If we know when darkness will come we can switch on streetlights and car headlights.
This makes our roads safer.
Sunrise and sunset come at a slightly different time each day.

Look at a daily paper every day to check these times.
Do the times change?
Keep a record.

Day and Date	Sunrise	Difference	Sunset	Difference
Mon 1. April	6.33		7.36	
Tues 2. April	6.30	3 min earlier	7.38	2 min later
Wed 3. April				

When the Sun goes down we need light to see and
heat to keep us warm.

We cannot see the Sun at night but we can see its light shining on the Moon.

MOONSHINE

The Moon takes almost a month to move round the Earth. Each night it seems to change shape.

Watch the Moon and make a **frieze** to show its changes.
As the Moon travels round the Earth the bright side begins to show.
First we see a tiny **crescent**.
This grows each night until it is a silvery **disc**.
The Moon moves on and we see its light fade to a crescent again.

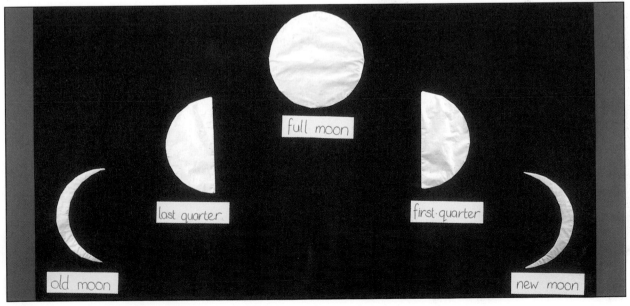

full moon

last quarter

first-quarter

old moon

new moon

TIME TACTICS

In our busy world people work both day and night.
Footballers sometimes play after dark.
Ambulance drivers take injured people to hospital during the night or the day.
Bakers make bread at night to sell fresh first thing in the morning.

The pilot is flying the aeroplane at night.
In the dark, the runway is lit up by lights so that the aeroplane can land in the right place.
Many people work in airports at night to make sure that aeroplanes can take off and land safely.

Talk to lots of people.
Do they work by day, at night, or sometimes both?

Job	Day	Evening	Night
Policeman/woman	✓	✓	✓
Chef	✓	✓	
Shop assistant	✓		

People who have finished their day's work enjoy watching the play.
Many people, like actors, have to work at night.

This moth likes the dark.
It can feed on honeysuckle flowers, which open at night.

NIGHTSPOT

Some **insects** and **minibeasts** love the dark.
Some enjoy the daylight.

It's easy to spot the sun-lovers.
Look for butterflies, ladybirds and spiders.
Do some moths like the sun too?

Make a minibeast trap.
Bury a jam jar in a shady
place at the end of the
day.
Put a stone or small
branch either side with
a brick resting on top.
Look in the morning to
see what creatures have
fallen into your trap. Let
them go.

Keep a diary of the creatures you catch in your trap.

Monday
earwig
beetle
centipede

Tuesday
slug
beetle

Badgers sleep during the day. At night they hunt for worms, insects and small **mammals**.

NIGHT PATROL

While we are fast asleep many creatures are busy.
Bats catch moths. Owls use their sharp eyes to spot
mice to eat.
Foxes chase rabbits or raid our dustbins.

Daytime

1. Starling   4. Human
2. Robin   5. Deer
3. Dog   6. Butterfly

Night-time

1. Owl   4. Fox
2. Bat   5. Mouse
3. Hedgehog   6. Moth

Look at these two pictures.
One shows creatures you might see in the daytime.
One shows the same place at night.
Look at the **keys** to match the creatures to the
numbers. How many of these creatures have you seen?
Find out more about them.

The daisies open their flowers wide in the sunshine.
Many insects are attracted to them.

OPEN AND SHUT CASE

Flowers can move!
When it is dark many flowers close for the night. There are few insects about.

In the bright daylight their beautiful **petals** open again.
Their sweet-smelling scent fills the air.
The insects call in for their food.

Plant some crocuses or daisies in two pots.

When they flower leave one pot in a dark cupboard.

Leave the other on a bright windowsill.

Look at your flowers at the end of the day.

Is there any difference between them?

STAR BRIGHT

Each star is a sun. Stars are far away.
At night they look like pinpricks of light.
Stars seem to make different patterns, which we call
constellations.

Copy this star pattern on to the bottom of a small
cardboard box.

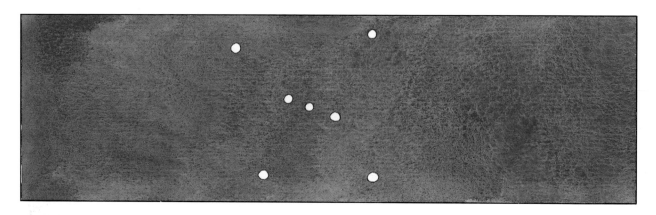

Ask an adult to make
holes for your stars with a
small nail.
Paint the box black
inside.
Cover the opening with
black paper and make
an eye hole.
Hold the box to the light
and look through your
star viewer to see your
stars by day.

Look at the stars. On a clear night we can see their light shining down to us on Earth.

Cats can be active at any time in the day or night.
They have naps whenever they feel tired.

SLEEP TIGHT

Human babies sleep a lot. They need time to rest and grow.
They wake up to be fed. It could be any time during the day or night.
As they get older they learn to sleep through the night.

We feel active during the day. We feel tired at night.
Everyone needs time to rest their body.
Some people seem to need more sleep than others.
Ask children and adults how much sleep they usually have each night.

Name	Bedtime	Get up	Sleep time
James	7.00pm	7.00am	12 hours
Ms Harris	11.00pm	7.00am	8 hours

Do children sleep more than adults?
Why do you think this is?

GLOSSARY

Constellations Star patterns as we see them from Earth.

Crescent Part of the outline of a round shape.

Digital timers Clocks or watches that display the time using figures rather than with hands on a dial.

Disc A flat, round shape.

Insects Creatures with six legs.

Key A list that tells you what is in a picture.

Mammals Animals that feed their babies with milk.

Minibeasts Small creatures that live in or under the soil.

Petals The coloured parts of a flower.

Shadows Dark shapes made by objects that block the light.

Sundial A clock that uses sunlight and shadow to measure time.

FINDING OUT MORE

Books to read:

Light and Dark by Ed Catherall (Wayland, 1989)
My Day series by Roger Coote and Diana Bentley (Firefly, 1989)
My Shadow by Sheila Gore (A & C Black, 1989)
Time by John Williams (Wayland, 1990)
What Makes Day and Night by Franklyn M Branley (A & C Black, 1989)

PICTURE ACKNOWLEDGEMENTS

Bruce Coleman 20; Eye Ubiquitous 10; Tony Stone Worldwide 18, 29; Topham 7, 8, 13; Wayland Picture Library 15, 19, (Zul Mukhida) cover, 5, 6, 9, 11, 12, 14, 17, 21, 25, 26; ZEFA 4, 15, 16, 22, 24, 27, 28.
Artwork illustrations by Rebecca Archer.
The publishers would also like to thank Davigdor Infants School and The Fold School, Hove, East Sussex, and St. Bernadette's First School, Brighton, East Sussex, for their kind cooperation.

INDEX

Babies 29
Badgers 22
Bats 23

Clocks 11, 12–13

Darkness 14, 18, 21, 25
Digital 12

Earth 5, 6, 17, 27

Flowers 20, 24–5
Foxes 23

Globe 5

Insects 21, 22, 24, 25

Light 5, 14–15, 16, 18, 21, 25, 26, 27

Mice 23
Minibeasts 21

Moon 16–17
Moths 20, 23

Owls 23

Rabbits 23

Sand-glass 10–11
Shadows 6, 7, 8, 9
Sleep 23, 28–9
Star viewer 26
Stars 26–7
Summer 14
Sun 5, 6, 11, 15, 16, 21
Sundial 8, 9
Sunrise 14
Sunset 14

Time 8–9, 11, 12–13
Twenty-four hour clock 12

Winter 14
Work 18–19